IZAAK WALTON

*from a painting by J. Huysmans in the
National Portrait Gallery.*

IZAAK
WALTON

by MARGARET BOTTRALL

PUBLISHED FOR

THE BRITISH COUNCIL

and the NATIONAL BOOK LEAGUE

BY LONGMANS, GREEN & CO., LONDON, NEW YORK, TORONTO

LONGMANS GREEN & CO. LTD.
6 & 7 Clifford Street, London W.1
Boston House, Strand Street, Cape Town
531 Little Collins Street, Melbourne

LONGMANS, GREEN & CO. INC.
55 Fifth Avenue, New York 3

LONGMANS, GREEN & CO.
20 Cranfield Road, Toronto 16

ORIENT LONGMANS LTD.
Calcutta Bombay Madras
Delhi Vijayawada Dacca

First published in 1955

Printed in Great Britain at The Curwen Press, Plaistow, E13

CONTENTS

¶ Izaak Walton was born at Stafford, probably on 9 August 1593. He died on 15 December 1683 and is buried in Winchester Cathedral.

IZAAK WALTON

I

THE MENTION of Izaak Walton's name immediately suggests *The Compleat Angler*, the contemplative man's
recreation, the peaceful fisherman, book in hand, depicted
in the memorial window in Winchester Cathedral. It seems
almost treasonable to allege that the extraordinary popularity
of the book has resulted in a distorted picture of its author;
but extraordinary is the mildest word that can be applied to
its reputation. Its real vogue only began when Walton had
been in his grave for well over a hundred years. True, it was
well received, and was re-issued, with various alterations and
additions, four times during his life; but it then had to wait
more than seventy years to be rescued from obscurity, and
it was not till after 1823 that the spate of re-issues began in
earnest. Whereas in the eighteenth century there were only
ten editions of the book, in the nineteenth there were a
hundred and fifty-nine, and in the first half of the twentieth
century more than a hundred reprints have appeared. *The
Compleat Angler* is more than a minor classic; in its way it is
a best-seller. The ingredients of the book—its combination
of practical advice with pastoral fantasy and good-humoured
piety—are of a kind to commend it, even today, to English
palates; and among the devotees of Walton are a number of
readers who might not relish so heartily works of greater
literary pretensions.

To Walton himself the book was, explicitly, a recreation,
written during the Cromwellian ascendancy to solace himself for the loss of happy bygone days. The work to which
he devoted much patient labour through many years was
the compilation of his five *Lives*; and these received on their
appearance quite as warm a welcome as that accorded to
The Compleat Angler. Each single Life was re-issued more
than once during Walton's lifetime (Hooker's no less than
six times) and he continued to enlarge and correct his

biographies until he was satisfied that they were as good as he could make them. That they were published collectively in 1670 (another edition of this volume appearing five years later) demonstrates that they were recognized as having merits quite beyond those of the ordinary prefatory Life. Primarily Walton was an amateur historian, whose lively interest in the fortunes of the Church of England and in the personalities of some of her illustrious sons was matched by his diligence in accumulating material for their biographies. Only incidentally was he a fisherman; he was not even a very great authority on angling.

If *The Compleat Angler* had been, from a professional point of view, an exhaustive treatise, it would not have been necessary for Charles Cotton to supplement it in 1676 with 'Instructions how to angle for a Trout or Grayling in a Clear Stream', or for Colonel Venables in the same year to add, with Walton's approval, a third section. Nor did *The Compleat Angler* at its first appearance fill a long-felt want, for two years previously, in 1651, Thomas Barker had published his little handbook, *The Art of Angling*, reprinted as *Barker's Delight* in 1653, 1654, 1657 and 1659. Walton's own angling editor, R. B. Marston, admits that Barker was Walton's superior as a fly-fisher, and that his experience was far more varied. He was, moreover, an enthusiastic cook, and included a number of excellent recipes in his book. Walton, who acknowledges his debt to Barker, very sensibly followed his example in this respect, and cheerfully drew on him and on earlier handbooks on angling to supplement his own first-hand experience. He also incorporated all sorts of fabulous lore in *The Compleat Angler*, thus drawing down upon himself the wrathful contempt of a Cromwellian trooper named Richard Franck, whose *Northern Memoirs*, compiled in 1658, prove him to have been an expert fisherman, even if a pedantic and disagreeable person. Franck says that Walton 'lays the stress of his arguments upon other men's observations, wherewith he stuffs his indigested octavo'; and when it is suggested that *The Compleat Angler*

'may pass muster among common mudlers', the curt re-
joinder is, 'No, I think not'. Franck seems to stand alone in
his insensibility to the charm of the book, which lies precisely
in the fact that it is the production of an amateur. Its aim is
quite as much to delight as to instruct, and its merits lie
more in its digressions and fanciful disquisitions than in its
usefulness as a fisherman's manual. There is enough sound,
practical experience included in it to commend it to actual
anglers, but it excels in being a conspicuously friendly book,
in which an enthusiast is seeking to persuade others to share
his various enjoyments.

II

It was by chance, not training, that Walton became a
writer. Had Sir Henry Wotton fulfilled his intention of
writing a Life of Donne and 'a Discourse of the Art, and in
praise of Angling', it is possible that Walton might never
have ventured into literature. His references to his education
and to his fitness to chronicle the lives of distinguished men
are always deprecating, and the little we know of his origins
shows that he was a man who rose quite remarkably above
the social setting into which he was born.

His father, Gervase Walton, was an alehouse-keeper in the
neighbourhood of Stafford; his mother, Anne, whose maiden
name has not been traced, married another Stafford inn-
keeper in 1598, a year after the death of Izaak's father, when
the little boy was five years old. He was baptized at St.
Mary's, Stafford, on 21 September 1593, and his birth-date
has often been assumed to be 9 August, which is the date, in
his ninetieth year, when he began to draft his Will. Nothing
is known of his childhood and schooling, and one wishes
that he, with his insatiable interest in personal anecdote, had
thought it worth while to preserve, if only for his descen-
dants, a record of his upbringing and early life. Somehow he
acquired a love of books, and the ability to express himself

with ease and grace; his script was beautiful and scholarly, though his spelling was eccentric, even by seventeenth-century standards.

By the time he was twenty he was in London, apprenticed to a kinsman, Thomas Grinsell. The tradition that Walton was some kind of a clothier has been confirmed by the recent discovery of records describing Grinsell as a sempster and Walton as a draper. He appears to have rented half a shop in Fleet Street and to have lived in Chancery Lane. In 1618 he was admitted a free brother of the Ironmongers' Company, to which Grinsell also belonged, and in the licence for his first marriage he is described as 'of the Cittie of London Ironmonger'. By 1637 the Company had appointed him Warden of their Yeomanry. This connection does not imply that he was ever engaged in the ironmongery trade. Donne's father had at one time been Warden of this same Company, and this may possibly have been one of the links which drew the two men together when Donne became Vicar of St. Dunstan's in the West, a living which he held, in conjunction with the Deanery of St. Paul's, from 1624 until the time of his death. This was Walton's parish church, and he held various parochial offices, including that of vestryman.

There is evidence that as quite a young man Walton was interested in literature, for a volume of verse, *The Loves of Amos and Laura*, by one S.P., was dedicated to him in 1619, with very flattering lines suggesting that he was a connoisseur of poetry if not a poet himself. Enough of Walton's occasional verse has survived to make this plausible; although it never rises above mediocrity, it is sufficiently accomplished to suggest that he had practised the craft with some diligence and discrimination.

In 1626 Izaak Walton married, at Canterbury, Rachel Floud, who was maternally descended from Archdeacon Cranmer, brother of the Archbishop. Her uncle, George Cranmer, had been one of Hooker's favourite pupils at Oxford, and an aunt had married Hooker's literary executor, John Spencer, President of Corpus Christi College, Oxford.

If Walton was not already moving in clerical circles, his marriage connected him with them. Rachel Walton bore him seven children, all of whom died young, she herself dying in 1640. It was in this year that Walton's *Life of Dr. Donne* was published, prefacing an edition of his Sermons. Sir Henry Wotton, who had intended to write a commemorative Life of Donne, had himself died in 1639. Walton's many bereavements may have impelled him to move his house and business. His name disappears from the registers of St. Dunstan's after 1644, but he seems to have remained in London.

By this time he was evidently a quite well-to-do man, for in 1643 he had paid £30 in parliamentary levies, and in 1646 he lent £50 to Edmund Carew of the Inner Temple—substantial sums in seventeenth-century currency. Later in his life he was described in legal documents as 'Gentleman', though on the title-page of the fifth edition of *The Compleat Angler*, the last that Walton revised, a careful differentiation is made between 'Mr. Izaak Walton' and 'Charles Cotton, Esq.'.

In 1646 Walton married, at Clerkenwell, Anne Ken, whose young half-brother Thomas was later to become the famous bishop and hymn-writer. There were three children of this marriage, two of whom survived, a son Isaac and a daughter Anne.

After the defeat of the royalist forces at Worcester in 1651 occurred the one episode in Walton's career which has a touch of excitement in it. One of Prince Charles's jewels, the lesser George, which had been hidden for safety by a royalist officer taken prisoner near Stafford, was eventually conveyed to the same officer, by now in the Tower, 'by the trusty hands of Mr. Isaac Walton'. The Waltons appear to have lived for a while in the neighbourhood of Stafford about this time, when London was an unpleasant place for shopkeepers of outspoken royalist sympathies; but the publication of the *Life of Sir Henry Wotton* in 1651 and of *The Compleat Angler* in 1653 suggests that Walton was not away for long.

After the Restoration (which moved him to write a joyful eclogue) he was appointed Steward to Dr. Morley, who was Bishop of Worcester from 1660–2. Mrs. Walton died in the latter year, and was buried in Worcester Cathedral, with a touching epitaph composed by her husband. When Morley was transferred to the see of Winchester, Walton went with him. Whether he continued to act as his Steward is not certainly known, but he undoubtedly spent a great deal of his time at Farnham Castle, and was on the best of terms with the Bishop. It was with Morley's encouragement, though at the bidding of Bishop Sheldon, that Walton published his *Life of Mr. Richard Hooker* in 1665. Five years later he brought out his *Life of Mr. George Herbert*, the one life that seems to have been written at nobody's instigation, though it may be that his acquaintance at Worcester with Barnabas Oley, Herbert's editor, gave him the impetus to celebrate the man he so much admired.

The year that saw the publication of the *Life of Herbert* saw also a collected edition of the four *Lives* that had been written up to this date. In 1678, when Walton was eighty-five, he brought out the *Life of Dr. Robert Sanderson*, which is scarcely inferior to the others in spite of the author's great age. Dr. Morley had urged him to undertake this task, and helped him with his reminiscences.

Walton's later life seems to have been very serene. His son Isaac went to Oxford and took holy orders, travelling abroad with Ken for a while, and eventually becoming a Canon of Salisbury. His daughter Anne married William Hawkins, a prebendary of Winchester, who was also rector of Droxford, a parish in the neighbourhood. The old man made his home with them and his grandchildren in both places.

In his ninetieth year he was responsible for bringing out a poem, *Thealma and Clearchus*, by John Chalkhill, some of whose verses are quoted in *The Compleat Angler*. This occasion drew from Thomas Flatman some pleasant lines addressed to Walton:

Happy old man, whose worth all mankind knows
Except himself, who charitably shows
The ready road to Virtue and to Praise,
The road to many long, and happy days;
The noble arts of generous piety,
And how to compass true felicity.
. . . he knows no anxious cares,
Thro' near a Century of pleasant years;
Easy he lives, and cheerful shall he die,
Well spoken of by late posterity.

Walton's will, drawn up when he was ninety, is a characteristic document. By this time he owned two houses in London, a cottage near Stafford and a farm near Winchester. All his property is most carefully disposed of, his favourite books (foremost among them Donne's *Sermons*) being specially mentioned. He remembered his native town in various benefactions, including a bequest of money

> to buie coles for some pore people, that shall most neide them in the said towne; the saide coles to be delivered the last weike in Janewary, or in every first weike in Febrewary: I say then, because I take that time to be the hardest and most pinching times with pore people.

Among various small bequests, his son is asked to look after his 'Ante Beacham' and to allow her 'about fiftie shilling a yeare in or for bacon and cheise (not more)'. He left many mourning rings as tokens to his friends, among them one for Bishop Morley with the posy 'A mite for a million'. Three months after making this will, Izaak Walton died, on 15 December 1683, during a great frost, and his remains were buried in Winchester Cathedral.

The two portraits of Walton that have come down to us confirm the impression which we get from all his writings. Here is a strong, honest, humorous and serious man; a man both shrewd and kindly. He may have been inferior in birth, education and opportunity to many of the men with whom he associated, but his face alone would testify against his being a pious sycophant, as some of his hostile critics have suggested. Rather it bears out the remark of Charles Cotton:

'My father Walton will be seen twice in no man's company he does not like, and likes none but such as he believes to be very honest men.'

Among such honest men and firm friends were John Donne, who sent to Walton (as he did to George Herbert) one of his specially designed emblematic seals—with which both Izaak Waltons, father and son, successively signed their own wills. There was Henry King, Bishop of Chichester, another recipient of a Donne seal, himself a fine poet, whose friendly letter prefixed to the *Life of Hooker* speaks of 'a Familiarity of more then Forty years continuance, and the constant experience of your Love, even in the worst of the late sad times'. There was Sir Henry Wotton, the renowned diplomatist, poet, and Provost of Eton, who not only went fishing with Walton but enlisted his help in various literary projects. There were, among many others, Michael Drayton the poet, William Cartwright the dramatist, Dr. John Hales of Eton, the distinguished physician Dr. Thomas Warton, Charles Cotton, another considerable poet and something of a rake, besides a bevy of bishops and ecclesiastics, among whom George Morley, the Bishop of Winchester, was certainly the closest friend and the intermediary by whom Walton got to know so large a clerical circle.

Such men would not have honoured Walton with their friendship if they had not found in him a singular degree of integrity and intelligence. As for his geniality, that smiles out from every page of *The Compleat Angler*, and is often to be discerned in the *Lives*, though they are pitched in a sober key. Without ever intruding himself, Walton manages to convey to his readers his personal feelings, whether of enjoyment of his pastime or of veneration and affection for the subjects of his biographies, and thus he leaves an indelible impression of his own disposition.

III

Walton's religious and political sympathies were strong and undeviating. His conduct and his associates prove him a staunch Anglican and Royalist, and naturally his writings bear this out. Especially interesting in this connection are the two Letters published in 1680 under the title *Love and Truth*. Walton did not publicly acknowledge their parentage, but the internal evidence that he wrote them is overwhelming.[1] They purport to be written 'from a quiet and conformable citizen of London, to two busie and factious shopkeepers in Coventry' and both deal with 'the distemper of the present times'. The first, written in 1667, taxes the Dissenters with fostering schism and sedition, and argues that the penalties enforced against them are no more severe and no less justified than they were 'in the very happy days of our late and Good Queen Elizabeth'. It defends the Anglican form of public worship, and begs the Nonconformist busybodies to repent their indiscreet zeal and 'study to be quiet' (one of Walton's favourite scriptural quotations).

The second Letter, written some twelve years later, is more humorous and unmistakably Waltonian.[2] Conceding that all the faults are not on one side, it gives a glimpse of the Restoration cleric 'in a long, curled, trim *Periwig*, a large *Tippet*, and a silk *Cassock*', and of clergy wives 'striving for Precedency and for the highest places in Church Pews', decked out in 'silk Cloaths, be-daub'd with lace, and their heads hanged about with painted Ribands'. Nevertheless, the author rejoices at having been bred in the Church of England, and warns his correspondents to be on their guard against Papists, who would be the chief gainers if there were a schism between the Anglicans and the Dissenters. If Popery came back, 'farewell the liberty and care of tender Consciences; there would be an end of that cajoling and flattery'. In very similar terms to those which Walton uses in the *Life of Hooker*, the women and shopkeepers 'and the middle-witted people' of 'this sinful Nation' are warned against

---

[1] Included by Zouch in his third edition of the *Lives* (1817) and by G. L. Keynes in the *Collected Works of Izaak Walton*, Nonesuch Press, 1929.

[2] Archbishop Sancroft, in his copy now in the Library of Emmanuel College, Cambridge, attributes the Letters to Izaak Walton.

meddling in 'Divinity, and the Government of the *Church and State*'. There is another account of Anglican church services, and a defence of the prayer-book, 'so pathetically and properly worded'. Charles I is extolled as a pattern of the Christian graces, and the author laments that 'Almighty God hath appointed me to live in an Age, in which Contention increases and Charity decays'.

It is not often, even in the *Lives*, which gave him ample opportunity to reflect on the mysteries of change and chance and death, that Walton makes any comment that seems to spring from a deep religious experience. There is a fine passage in the *Life of Hooker*:

> Affliction is a Divine diet, which though it be not pleasing to Mankind, yet Almighty God hath often, very often, imposed it as good, though bitter Physick, to those children whose Souls are dearest to him.

Such aphorisms are, however, exceptional in Walton. No reader of the *Lives* can doubt that he was a thoughtful and sensitive man, but his reflections usually led him to accepted conclusions. He was a conformist who neither asked awkward questions himself nor approved of those who did. He is at his best when he recommends thankfulness, humility and patience as Christian duties; but sometimes his devout simplicity is combined with a good deal of sententiousness. This is markedly so in the long discourse on the duty of thankfulness which leads up to the conclusion of *The Compleat Angler* in its revised version. Piscator wishes his scholar to join him

> in thankfulness to the Giver of every good and perfect gift, for our happiness. And that our present happiness may appear to be the greater, and we the more thankful for it, I will beg you to consider with me how many do, even at this very time, lie under the torment of the stone, the gout, and tooth-ache; and this we are free from. And every misery I miss is a new mercy; and therefore let us be thankful.

Though Walton's church-going, conforming type of piety may seem dull and limited when it is contrasted with the spiritual agonies and ecstasies of his contemporaries George Fox or John Bunyan, it must in justice be remembered that he lived through a period when the steadfastness of devout Anglicans was thoroughly put to the test. Walton regarded all Dissenters as dangerous schismatics. His own respect for authority made it impossible for him to sympathize in the least with their pleas for liberty of conscience and the right of private judgement. Lay folk, in his opinion, should know their place. Several times in his writings he inveighs against the 'too many foolish meddlers in physick and divinity that think themselves fit to meddle with hidden secrets, and so bring destruction to their followers'. It cannot be doubted that the Church of England provided the right niche for a man of Walton's equable temperament and essentially reverent cast of mind.

IV

Throughout the *Lives* we find scattered remarks which betray Walton's nostalgia for the peaceful reign of James I. Though his loyalty to the monarchy was unquestionable, and though he celebrated the Restoration in rollicking stanzas, he realized that the England of his youth had vanished for ever. In 1665 he speaks of 'this weak and declining Age of the World', and as an old man, in the *Life of Sanderson*, he says:

> But when I look back upon the ruine of Families, the bloodshed, the decay of common honesty, and how the former piety and plain dealing of this now sinful Nation is turned into cruelty and cunning, I praise God that he prevented me from being of that party which help'd to bring in this Covenant, and those sad Confusions that have follow'd it.

Born in the year when Shakespeare's *Venus and Adonis* was published, Izaak Walton died a year after the publication of Dryden's *Religio Laici* and *MacFlecknoe*. Although most of his writing was done in the post-Restoration years, its spirit is of an earlier epoch. When in *The Compleat Angler* he introduces the pastoral songs of Marlowe and Ralegh, he remarks: 'They were old-fashioned poetry, but choicely good; I think much better than the strong lines that are now in fashion in this critical age.' The happy, tranquil tone of the whole book, with its many interludes of 'innocent, harmless mirth' may incline the reader to think of Walton as a belated Elizabethan; but its style and conception belong to a soberer age. It is worth remembering that Izaak Walton was born in the same year as George Herbert, though he survived him by half a century. Herbert by a merciful providence died before the outbreak of the great rebellion; Walton must sometimes have wished that he himself had lived no longer. Yet in spite of his heart-aches, he was evidently a happy old man, and certainly an uncommonly active and productive one.

The earliest extant piece by Walton is *An Elegy on Dr. Donne*, dated a week after Donne's death. This is more notable for its warmth of feeling than for genuine poetic merit, but it is interesting that Walton's first cry of lament is not for the loss that England has sustained of a man eminent in piety, but of a man

> where Language chose to stay
> And shew her utmost power. I would not praise
> That, and his great Wit, which in our vain days
> Make others proud: but, as these serv'd to unlock
> That Cabinet his mind, where such a stock
> Of knowledge was repos'd, that I lament
> Our just and general cause of discontent.

A fair number of Walton's songs and occasional verses have survived; those in *The Compleat Angler* are pleasantly adequate to the occasion, and so are his various dedicatory epistles and elegies; but prose was his proper medium.

He was a careful workman, and probably a slow one. The autograph manuscript of his notes for a *Life of John Hales* (written, it is true, when he was already eighty) is full of cancellations and emendations, suggesting that words and phrases did not flow freely from his pen. Nevertheless, Walton's finished style is remarkably flexible and unaffected. When he has facts to convey, he sets them down straight-forwardly; when he has a story to tell, he handles both narrative and digression with great skill; when there is need of a lyrical description or a piece of impressive eloquence, his style rises to the occasion. The famous peroration to the *Life of Donne* may be cited as an example of his finest, most impassioned prose:

> He was earnest and unwearied in the search of knowledge; with which his vigorous soul is now satisfied, and employed in a continual praise of that God that first breathed it into his active body; that body, which once was a *Temple of the Holy Ghost*, and is now become a small quantity of *Christian dust:*
> But I shall see it reanimated.

It may be worth remarking that the final word originally was 'reinanimated'. The correction of even single words in Walton's constant revisions is proof of his conscientious artistry.

No less carefully wrought, though altogether lighter and brighter in texture, is this passage from *The Compleat Angler:*

> But the Nightingale, another of my airy creatures, breathes such sweet loud musick out of her little instrumental throat, that it might make mankind to think miracles are not ceased. He that at midnight when the very labourer sleeps securely, should hear, as I have very oft, the clear airs, the sweet descants, the natural rising and falling, the doubling and redoubling of her voice, might well be lifted above earth and say, 'Lord, what musick hast thou provided for the Saints in Heaven, when thou affordest bad men such musick on Earth!'

Walton is fond of the balanced sentence, with alliteration used to stress the symmetry:

> Thus *variable*, thus *vertuous* was the Life: thus *excellent*, thus *exemplary* was the Death of this memorable man.

Another favourite device is his use of parenthesis, often for humorous effect. Walton's style is never intrusive, and his humorous asides are particularly unstressed, so that they sound almost demure, as in the comment:

> His late Majesty King *Charles* the *First*, that knew the value of Sir Henry *Wottons* pen, did by a perswasive loving violence (to which may be added the promise of 500 l. a year) force him to lay *Luther* aside, and betake himself to write the History of *England*.

In *The Compleat Angler*, Walton naturally allows his humour more play, and sometimes becomes quite frolicsome: 'If Mr. Pike be there, then the little fish will skip out of the water at his appearance.' But all in all, his is a sober, persuasive, lucid style, that seldom draws the reader's attention upon itself, but focuses it on the matter under discussion.

To appreciate Walton's mastery of extended narrative, it is of course essential to read at least one of the *Lives* in its entirety; but a good example of his anecdotal style can be extracted from the *Life of Sanderson*:

> About the time of his printing this excellent Preface, I met him accidentally in London in sad-coloured clothes, and God knows, far from being costly: the place of our meeting was near to *Little Britain*, where he had been to buy a book, which he then had in his hand: we had no inclination to part presently; and therefore turn'd to stand in a corner under a Penthouse (for it began to rain) and immediately the wind rose, and the rain increased so much, that both became so inconvenient as to force us into a cleanly house, where we had *Bread*, *Cheese*, *Ale* & a *Fire* for our money.

It is to the many anecdotes imbedded in them that the *Lives* owe much of their vivacity. Nobody who has read them will forget George Herbert's encounter with the carter on his way to the music-party at Salisbury, or Hooker's clerk protesting against the re-arrangement of the church furniture. In a few telling phrases, too, Walton can hit off a man's appearance or disposition; witness his account of Donne's 'winning behaviour (which when he would intice, had a strange kind of elegant, irresistible art)', and the glimpse of Hooker, so vivid though necessarily taken from hearsay: 'His Body worn out, not with Age, but Study and Holy Mortification; his Face full of Heat-pimples, begot by his inactivity and sedentary life.'

Walton's digressions are an essential part of his narrative technique, and he often draws attention to them by such remarks as:

> But the Reader may think that in this digression, I have already carried him too far from *Eaton-Colledge*, and therefore I shall lead him back as gently and as orderly as I may to that place, for a further conference concerning Sir *Henry Wotton*.

In this particular *Life*, some of the digressions might be called aimless, but usually Walton only leaves his main story in order to fill in the historical background or to give an account of someone closely connected with his chief character.

In *The Compleat Angler*, also a very digressive work, Walton shows such a fondness for the fabulous natural history derived from Pliny via Gesner and Topsel (whose *Foure-footed Beastes* appeared in 1607) that we might question whether so credulous a man could be a trustworthy biographer. He does mention that the Royal Society has listed thirty-three species of spider, and refers to the collections of contemporary naturalists, such as John Tradescant and Elias Ashmole; but where fishes or insects are concerned, he is quite content to accept and pass on all kinds of legendary information. For modern readers, of course, it is this unsophisticated and uncritical inclusiveness of Walton that constitutes one of the great charms of *The Compleat Angler*, combined as it so engagingly is with his accurate first-hand observation and practical knowledge. When he deals with the careers of men, Walton takes considerable pains to check his facts, and each one of his *Lives* was subjected to repeated revision.

V

This striving for perfection extended to *The Compleat Angler*, by-product though it was of his leisure hours. For the 1655 edition he practically re-wrote the version of 1653, increasing its length by about a third; and the final edition brought out under his own supervision, that of 1676, was a far more extensive affair than the first, containing as it did the supplements of Cotton and Venables. The additions to the original edition include several passages of conscious fine writing, and a great deal of moralizing; they make the treatise appear less of a handbook, and widen its appeal.

Formally, the book is a dialogue. There are, in the revised version, three speakers in the opening scene—the huntsman, the falconer and the angler. The falconer, having duly pleaded the merits of his sport, goes off to practice it; the hunter becomes a convert to the fisherman, and thereafter is addressed as 'scholar'. From time to time, minor characters —such as Maudlin the milkmaid and her mother, and the anglers Peter and Coridon—are introduced. When Walton has several people on the scene, he writes in a racy and colloquial way:

> *Piscator:* . . . Well met, gentlemen; this is lucky that we meet so just together at this very door. Come, hostess, where are you? is supper ready? Come, first give us a drink; and be as quick as you can, for I believe we are all very hungry. Well, brother Peter and Coridon, to you both! Come, drink: and then tell me what luck of fish: we two have caught but ten trouts, of which my scholar caught three. Look! Here's eight; and a brace we gave away. We have had a most pleasant day for fishing and talking, and are returned home both weary and hungry; and now meat and rest will be pleasant.

> *Peter:* And Coridon and I have not had an unpleasant day: and yet I have caught but five trouts; for, indeed, we went to a good honest ale-house, and there we played at shovel-board half the day; all the time that it rained we were there, and as merry as they that fished. And I am glad we are here now with a dry house over our heads; for hark! how it rains and blows . . .

For the major part of the book, the dialogue convention is abandoned in favour of long instructional speeches by Piscator; but when Walton suspects that his readers have had enough information, he introduces dialogue again, and sometimes puts his characters in motion:

> *Piscator:* ... But, come, now it hath done raining, let's stretch our legs a little in a gentle walk to the river, and try what interest our angles will pay us for lending them so long to be used by the Trouts; lent them indeed, like usurers, for our profit and their destruction.

> *Venator:* Oh me! look you, master, a fish! a fish! Oh, alas, master, I have lost her.

Another favourite device of Walton's to alleviate the weight of factual (or fabulous) description is to insert, on some pretext, a poem. *The Compleat Angler* includes verses by Marlowe, Ralegh, Donne, Drayton, Sir Henry Wotton, Du Bartas, George Herbert, Christopher Harvey, Phineas Fletcher and Waller, not to mention a number of less known names. Walton himself provides a cheerful catch and a 'composure' (or composition) entitled *The Angler's Wish*, which refers to the time he spent at Shallowford near Stafford with his second wife Anne Ken ('my Kenna').

In his prefatory Epistle to the Reader, Walton expressly says that he devised the book so that it should 'not read dull and tediously', seeing that the writing of it had been to him 'a recreation of a recreation'. He goes on:

> I am the willinger to justify the pleasant part of it, because though it is known I can be serious at seasonable times, yet the whole Discourse is, or rather was, a picture of my own disposition ...

This picture he provides by a characteristically modest and indirect method. He does not talk about the man Izaak Walton, but allows Piscator to be his mouthpiece. Piscator is not simply the champion and expositor of the art of angling; he is markedly pious, a considerable moralizer, a man who relishes verse and song as well as good food and drink, a great lover of the countryside, above all a man of tranquil and contented temper.

Walton's piety is so pervasive that it scarcely needs illustrating. His duty to God is never very far from his mind. His reliance on the Bible is exemplified in a most disarming way in the arguments which Piscator uses in defence of angling against the counter-attractions of hunting and hawking. He reminds his hearers of Christ's close fellowship with fishermen and of his miracles in connection with fish. Jonah is not forgotten—'Almighty God is said to have spoken to a fish, but never to a beast'. He conjectures that the prophet Amos was not only a shepherd, but a fisherman too, for his 'humble, lowly, plain style' reminds him of 'the affectionate, loving, lowly, humble Epistles of St. Peter, St. James and St. John, whom we know were all fishers': these he compares with 'the glorious language and high metaphors of St. Paul, who we may believe was not'.

No writer is more thoroughly English than Walton; and that, presumably, is why the English reading public took *The Compleat Angler* so warmly to their hearts, lavishing on it an abundance of praise that may be perplexing to foreign readers. Walton's delight in his favourite sport commends him, in the first place, to all amateurs; even non-fishermen can share in the enjoyment with which he expounds the mysteries of his craft. Next, he is a genuine lover of country sights and sounds, and it is well known that town-bred Englishmen often have a hankering for the countryside that is not shared by urban Europeans. Lastly, the Angler himself embodies the temperamental qualities on which Englishmen place a perhaps inordinate value; he is a kindly, tolerant, humorous, patient old man, who interferes with nobody, and who asks nothing better than to be allowed to enjoy his hobby in peace.

The reader who has never angled in his life may yet be beguiled by Walton's descriptions of the different kinds of fresh-water fish and of the bait and flies by which they may be taken, for he speaks of all created things—even grubs and caddis-worms—with a hearty appreciation of their natural qualities. He is very far, however, from restricting himself to the description of what he has actually observed. Some of his speculations remind us of the 'unnatural natural history' of *Euphues*. The slow growth and great size of the carp suggest to him comparisons with the bear, the elephant and the crocodile; he adduces authority for the belief that pike are bred from pickerel weed, quotes Pliny on the generation of caterpillars from dew-drops, and tells us (this time perhaps with his tongue in his cheek) that

> a person of honour, now living in Worcestershire, assured me that he had seen a necklace, or collar of tadpoles, hang like a chain or necklace of beads about a Pike's neck, and to kill him; whether it were for meat or malice, must be, to me, a question.

When, however, Walton has his eye on the object, he sets it before his readers with deft and vivid touches:

> The Minnow hath . . . a kind of dappled or waved colour, like to a panther, on its sides, inclining to a greenish or sky colour.

Walton's descriptions of nature are sometimes so artfully contrived that we are transported into Arcadia rather than to the banks of the Lea or the Thames. Some years before he wrote *The Compleat Angler*, he had tried his hand at pastoral fantasy, in the brief introduction which he wrote to Francis Quarles's *The Shepheards Oracles*. Though his style is more parenthetical and clumsy than in the later book, the idyllic note is the same:

> He in a Sommer's morning (about that howre when the great eye of Heaven first opens it selfe to give light to us mortals) walking a gentle pace towards a Brook (whose Spring-head was not far distant from his peacefull habitation) fitted with Angle, Lines and Flyes: Flyes proper for that season (being the fruitful month of *May*); intending to beguile the timrous Trout (with which that wat'ry element abounded) observ'd a more than common concourse of Shepheards . . .

There were shepherdesses, too, 'strewing the footpaths with Lillies, and Ladysmocks, so newly gathered by their fair hands, that they smelt more sweet then the morning . . .' This vein is exploited in *The Compleat Angler*, notably in Venator's long musing on the nature of true riches. Though this deserves to be quoted in its entirety, an extract must serve to indicate the quality of Walton's deliberately pastoral writing:

> I could there sit quietly; and looking on the water, see some fishes sport themselves in the silver streams, others leaping at flies of several shapes and colours; looking on the hills, I could behold them spotted with woods and groves; looking down the meadows, could see, here a boy gathering lilies and ladysmocks, and there a girl cropping culverkeys and cowslips, all to make garlands suitable to this present month of May.

No less delightful than these elaborations are the brief references to 'yonder high honey-suckle hedge' or to the rain-washed grass—'how pleasantly that meadow looks; nay, and the earth smells so sweetly, too'. Piscator and his pupil, for all their flights of eloquence, move in a country-side that is recognizably English.

> About All-hallantide, and so till frost comes, when you see men ploughing up heath ground, or greenswards, then follow the plough, and you shall find a white worm, as big as two maggots, and it hath a red head: you may observe in what ground most are, for there the crows will be very watchful and follow the plough very close . . .

They speak with warm approval of inns where they have been well treated, like the Thatched House at Hoddesdon; they expect from their hostesses comfortable beds, where 'the linen looks white, and smells of lavender', besides demanding plenty of good drink and excellent cooking. Walton's relish for well-cooked food is unmistakable and endearing:

Come, my friend Coridon, this Trout looks lovely; it was twenty-two inches when it was taken; and the belly of it looked, some part of it, as yellow as a marigold, and part of it as white as a lily; and yet, methinks, it looks better in this good sauce.

For all his moralizing, Piscator is a thoroughly likeable old fellow, and so, we conclude, was Izaak Walton; but we must remember that he was a man of many dimensions, whereas his Angler has but one.

It is for his literary craftsmanship that Walton is truly remarkable, not for his skill as a fisherman, or for his homely piety and quiet contentment. He could not write a handbook on his favourite sport without making it a kind of anthology of his delights, and lovingly revising it paragraph by paragraph; and the *Lives* he took very much more seriously.

VI

The spirit in which he approached the task of biographer reveals itself in the Introduction to the *Life of Hooker*, where he speaks of its preparation as 'a work of much labour to enquire, consider, research and determine what is needful to be known concerning him'. There can be no doubt of his 'well-meaning and diligence' when we note how he supplements personal recollections (either his own or those of persons well acquainted with his heroes) by references to records, letters and wills. When he can ascertain an exact date, he gives it, and his constant revisions show his wish to make his biographies as full and accurate as possible. The Appendix which he added to the *Life of Hooker* proves his anxiety in this respect. This Life probably gave him more trouble than any of the others, for not only was its subject a very eminent man, he also belonged to a generation of which there were almost no survivors at the time when Walton was writing.

It is probable that his interest in biography developed from the habit of collecting notes and anecdotes in the jackdaw spirit of Aubrey. We know from the *Life of Hooker* that he had begun to collect information about the great man at the time when he was first acquainted with the Cranmer family—that is, at the time of his first marriage, some forty years before Bishop Sheldon commissioned him to write a Life that should be a corrective to Gauden's memoir. Walton must have kept a diary of sorts, unless he had an absolutely prodigious memory for dates and conversations. But if the *Lives* owe their origin to an antiquarian's interest in the details relating to famous worthies, it is to an artist's conscious skill in the manipulation of his material that they owe their enduring merit.

Walton's attitude to all five of his subjects is that of the portrait painter. He does not walk all around his subjects, observing them from every point of view; or if he does, this is a preliminary process. Having made up his mind which are the most striking lineaments in each man, and from what angle they appear to the best advantage, Walton sets up his easel and works steadily. He uses different techniques—with Wotton he is more impressionistic, with Hooker and Sanderson he pays special attention to the background—but always he feels himself at liberty to treat some facts as more relevant to his purpose than others. This explains the apparent disproportion in the *Lives* of Donne and Herbert, in which the emphasis is overwhelmingly on their latter years. Though all five *Lives* were commemorative tributes, these two especially were written in a spirit of veneration. Walton was not, however, a monumental mason, any more than he was an anatomist. His eulogies are worked into the texture of the extended study. While it is possible to pick out from the *Lives* anecdotes and digressions that can be enjoyed out of their context, it is impossible to extract epitomes of the characters of the men whom Walton is portraying. Until we have looked at each picture in its totality, we cannot get the impression that he was working to convey.

Walton never wilfully misleads, even when he takes liberties that would be impossible today. If he makes a synthesis of several letters of Donne, presenting them as one continuous epistle, he gives the reader due warning that it is 'an extract collected out of some few of his many Letters'. If he paraphrases passages from Herbert's works and presents them as speeches uttered by Herbert, he is acting on the same principle that he acknowledges in the Preface to the *Life of Sanderson*—an artistic principle, enabling him to add life and variety to his narrative: 'I have been so bold, as to paraphrase and say what I think he (whom I had the happiness to know well) would have said upon the same occasion.' Walton did not actually know Herbert, but he knew his writings intimately, and when he puts words into Herbert's mouth, they are always beautifully in character. We may, indeed, rely on Walton's honesty and regard for truth, even though later investigators have established his occasional inaccuracy about circumstance or chronology. When he issued his revised *Life of Donne* in 1658, he set forth plainly his intentions and methods as a biographer:

> I either speak of my own knowledge, or from the testimony of such as dare do any thing, rather than speak an untruth. And for that part of it which is my own observation or opinion, if I had a power I would not use it to force any man's assent, but leave him a liberty to disbelieve what his own reason inclines him to.

Walton succeeds in investing all five of his *Lives* with a sense of intimacy because he so consistently relies on personal testimony. Donne and Wotton had been his friends, and Bishop Morley had made him acquainted with Dr. Sanderson; but Herbert he had only seen once, and Hooker had died while Walton was a child. These two *Lives*, however, are not inferior to the others in verisimilitude, for Walton turned for information about Herbert to men who had known him well, including Edmund Duncon and Arthur Woodnoth, who visited Herbert at Bemerton, and the man who ordained him, Dr. Humphrey Henchman, who 'tells me, He laid his hand on *Mr. Herberts* Head, and (alas!) within less then three years, lent his Shoulder to carry his dear Friend to his Grave'. Donne, too, may have talked about Herbert, whom he had known from childhood, and so may Henry King, who had been Herbert's schoolfellow at Westminster. Barnabas Oley, too, who included a brief account of Herbert in his edition of *A Priest to the Temple*, was Treasurer of Worcester Cathedral at the time when Walton was Bishop Morley's steward there. For the *Life of Hooker* he drew upon the information he had collected years earlier, at the time of his connection with the Cranmer family and Dr. John Spencer; he mentions also his conversations with Archbishop Usher, Bishop Morton, and 'the learned John Hales of Eaton-Colledge', all of whom 'loved the very name of Mr. Hooker'.

Walton was very far, however, from being a mere retailer of personal gossip. There are some notes extant which he sent to John Aubrey, who had asked for his recollections of Ben Jonson. He confesses that he scarcely knew him, but supplies some reminiscences that Bishop Morley, in conversation, had summoned up, making quite clear that none of the material is more than hearsay. Even when Walton could speak at first hand, and might legitimately have introduced himself into the narrative, his sense of decorum made him refrain. For example, we know from *The Compleat Angler* that he used to go fishing with Sir Henry Wotton, and had many discourses with him about the art of angling; but in the *Life of Wotton*, we find only this passage:

> Nor did he forget his innate pleasure of *Angling*, which he would usually call, *his idle time, not idly spent*: saying often, he would rather live five *May months*, then forty *Decembers*.

A still more striking example of self-effacement may be observed in the *Life of Donne*. From the letter which Bishop King, one of Donne's executors, wrote many years later to 'Honest Izaak', it appears that Walton was present at Donne's bedside three days before his death, when the Dean entrusted his Sermons to his friend King; but Walton himself makes no mention of the incident. His love and veneration for Donne were too great to allow him to intrude himself into his deeply moving account of the great man's

last days on earth. Notwithstanding Walton's regard for
personal testimony and first-hand observation, he was no
Boswell, rushing in where angels fear to tread. His attitude
has more in common with that of John Roper, who in his
Life of his father-in-law Sir Thomas More conveys a won-
derful sense of intimacy without sacrifice of reverence.

Walton has been criticized for an excess of reverence
towards the subjects of his biography, and also for reducing
them all to a sameness of gentle piety. Certainly he took no
liberties with any of them, but it would have been as much
against the conventions of his age as against his own good
instincts if he had done so. It is true that he celebrates
Dr. Donne the Dean of St. Paul's and pays scant attention to
Jack Donne the poet and amorist; true that he spends far
more time on the three years of Herbert's pastorate at
Bemerton than on the rest of his career. But he was com-
memorating in both men the qualities and achievements
which they themselves would have wished to endure in the
minds of posterity. By the time of his death, Donne's fame
as a divine and preacher had made the exploits of his youth
seem of little account. Walton was not in the least idiosyn-
cratic in valuing his sermons and sacred poems, together with
his theological and devotional prose writings, far above the
poems which during his lifetime he had never troubled to
collect, some of which he would gladly have disowned.
Walton's own verdict is made quite explicit in the lines
which he wrote for the 1635 edition of Donne's poems.
They appeared beneath William Marshall's portrait of Donne
at eighteen, and run:

> This was for youth, Strength, Mirth and wit that Time
> Most count their golden Age: but t'was not thine.
> Thine was thy later yeares, so much refind
> From youth's Drosse, Mirth & wit; as thy pure mind
> Thought (like the Angels) nothing but the Praise
> Of thy Creator, in those last, best Dayes.
>   Witnes this Booke, (thy Embleme) which begins
>   With Love; but endes, with Sighes, & Teares for sins.

Walton could scarcely have anticipated that in three hundred years' time both Donne and Herbert would owe their reputation primarily to their poetry. He saw them, as all his contemporaries did, as ornaments of the Anglican church. If he regarded them both with veneration, he did not, in fact, minimize the contrast between Donne's headstrong, unsettled youth and the penitential gravity of his later years, any more than he failed to record young Herbert's ambitions of worldly success.

It is in the *Life of Sir Henry Wotton*, delightful as it is in its rambling way, that Walton's limitations are most clearly seen. He had not the experience of the world to enable him to write an adequate biography of a very remarkable diplomatist and statesman. He could appreciate the scholarly and pious aspects of Wotton's character, but could not convey his brilliance. The *Life* was apparently written in haste in order to serve as a preface to the *Reliquiae Wottonianae* which were published in 1651 (and frequently reprinted). Walton apologizes for his own shortcomings, but loyalty to the memory of a friend evidently operated as it did with the *Life of Donne*. Rather than see Donne's *Sermons* appear without a prefatory Life, Walton hastily wrote one. He and Wotton had been collecting the material for some time, but the actual composition seems to have taken Walton less than two months. Similarly, in default of a worthier Life to introduce Wotton's collected writings to the public, Walton supplied one.

The *Life of Mr. George Herbert* was written out of pure regard for 'that great example of holiness', and was printed as an independent biography, not attached to any edition of Herbert's works. The *Lives* of Hooker and Sanderson were both commissioned by bishops, and had a more polemical intention than the other three. Both men had contended at different epochs with the policies of puritan extremists, and in order to set their achievements in the right perspective, Walton related their individual careers to the general politico-religious background.

These two *Lives* are especially well documented. Walton's main authorities for the Elizabethan survey were Camden (to whom he refers constantly throughout the *Lives*) and Spotswood's *History of the Church of Scotland*. Fuller was another historian to whom he was indebted. He is usually careful to cite his sources. Conscientiousness, indeed, was the impelling force behind his practice of constant revision.

Walton had few English predecessors in the art of biography; indeed, the term 'biographer' first occurs in the 1660's, though 'historiographer' was current earlier. He lived, however, at a time when men's minds, besides turning inward to self-scrutiny, were pursuing the study of character through the observation of their fellows. Among Walton's contemporaries were the great introspectives, Bunyan, Fox, Sir Thomas Browne; there was Richard Baxter, who could look both inwards and outwards and report reliably on all his findings; there were the diarists, Pepys and Evelyn; and there was Clarendon, who was compiling his incomparable gallery of Civil War 'characters'; yet as an artist in pure biography, there is nobody in the seventeenth century to touch Izaak Walton.

He had, in the first place, an unusual appreciation of the value of factual material, and was a diligent searcher after dates and documents. He was not the first biographer to use letters, but he made an exceptionally intelligent use of them in his *Lives* of Donne and Herbert. (Incidentally, we owe to Walton the preservation of the two sonnets which the seventeen-year-old Herbert sent to his mother as a new-year gift.) Walton also realized that personal impressions were both immensely valuable and very perishable, and he accordingly took pains to include as many as he considered trustworthy.

He was much more, however, than a conscientious collector of biographical material, much more than an ingenious arranger of that material; he was an artist with a great gift of human sympathy. It is his own personal feeling of reverent affection that animates the studies of Donne, Wotton,

Hooker, Herbert and Sanderson, and unifies the five *Lives* that were written at such different times and for such different purposes. Subordinating himself completely, yet maintaining a consistent and characteristic point of view, Walton produced a series of portraits that were as true and as beautiful as he was able to make them. He excelled in the faculty which Dr. Johnson singled out for particular praise when he wrote in *The Rambler* of the art of the biographer (in which he was himself a master); the discrimination 'to pass slightly over those performances and incidents which produce vulgar greatness, to lead the thoughts into domestic privacies, and to display the minute details of daily life'. It is small wonder that Johnson reckoned Walton's *Lives* 'one of his most favourite books'.

In common with the *Lives*, *The Compleat Angler* also commended itself to Johnson's acute judgement, and it was at his instigation that Moses Browne rescued it from neglect and re-issued it in 1750. Sir John Hawkins, who ten years later brought out a more accurate edition, which included a life of Walton, was also a friend of Johnson's. The rather whimsical charm of the book, however, was only fully appreciated by a later generation. It was a volume after Charles Lamb's own heart, and none of its innumerable eulogists have praised it better. Recommending the book to Coleridge, he wrote: 'It breathes the very spirit of innocence, purity, and simplicity of heart; . . . it would sweeten a man's temper at any time to read it; it would Christianise every angry, discordant passion; pray make yourself acquainted with it.'

Since that time Izaak Walton has become the object of a cult. *The Compleat Angler* has been printed again and again, sometimes very sumptuously, and the little handbook written for his own pleasure to celebrate his favourite pastime has become Walton's chief guarantee of immortality. For the thousands of people who connect Walton's name with angling, only dozens have read the *Lives*.

Fate is apt to play odd tricks with a man's literary remains, so that what he valued most is left unread, and his unconsidered trifles are treasured. Something of the kind has happened with Donne, and we see it with Walton too. But whereas Donne's sermons and theological works call for a degree of perseverance which the twentieth-century reader is loath to give, Walton's serious works commend themselves by being brief and delightfully readable. Anyone who is attracted to 'honest Izaak' in the guise of Piscator will find his qualities displayed to even better advantage in the *Lives*; and he will also make the acquaintance, on intimate terms, of five very memorable worthies of the seventeenth century.

IZAAK WALTON

A Select Bibliography

(Place of publication London unless stated otherwise)

Bibliographies:

THE CHRONICLE OF THE COMPLEAT ANGLER, by T. Westwood (1864).
Reprinted with additions in R. B. Marston's Lea & Dove edition of
The Compleat Angler, 1888.

A BIBLIOGRAPHY OF THE COMPLEAT ANGLER, by A. Wood, New York
(1900).

A NEW CHRONICLE OF THE COMPLEAT ANGLER, by P. Oliver (1936).
Records 284 editions.

A BIBLIOGRAPHY OF IZAAK WALTON'S LIVES, by J. E. Butt, in *Proceedings
of the Oxford Bibliographical Society*, vol. 2 (1930).
Records only seventeenth-century editions.

Collected Works:

THE LIVES OF DR. JOHN DONNE, SIR HENRY WOTTON, MR. RICHARD
HOOKER, MR. GEORGE HERBERT (1670).
The Life of Dr. Sanderson was added to the edition of this collection
edited by T. Zouch, York, 1796.
Walton's *Lives* were reprinted in the World's Classics, 1927.

WALTONIANA, edited by R. H. Shepherd (1878).
Contains all but two of Walton's prose and verse remains.

THE COMPLEAT WALTON, edited by G. L. Keynes (1929).
A one-volume edition, with bibliographical notes, published by the
Nonesuch Press.

Separate Works:

THE LIFE AND DEATH OF DR. DONNE (prefixed to *LXXX Sermons*,
preached by . . . John Donne, 1640). *Biography*.
A second edition, enlarged, appeared separately in 1658 as *The Life
of John Donne*.

THE LIFE OF SIR HENRY WOTTON (prefixed to *Reliquiae Wottonianae*, 1651) (1651). *Biography*.
A second edition, with additions and alterations, appeared in the 1654 edition of *Reliquiae Wottonianae*.

THE COMPLEAT ANGLER or THE CONTEMPLATIVE MAN'S RECREATION (1653). *Sport*.
'Much enlarged' in 1655. Walton's last revision, 1676. The most authoritative editions are those by Sir H. Nicolas, 2 vols., 1836, which contains the best life of Walton, and by R. B. Marston, 2 vols., 1888.

THE LIFE OF MR. RICHARD HOOKER (1665). *Biography*.

THE LIFE OF MR. GEORGE HERBERT (1670). *Biography*.

THE LIFE OF DR. SANDERSON (1678). *Biography*.

LOVE AND TRUTH (1680). *Letters*.
Published anonymously.

Some Critical and Biographical Studies:

LIVES OF ENGLISH LAYMEN, by W. Teal (1842).
The work of a sententious clergyman, drawing on Sir Harris Nicolas and other editors of Walton's work.

IZAAK WALTON AND THE EARLIER ENGLISH WRITERS ON ANGLING, by G. M. Tweddell (1854).

WALTON AND SOME EARLIER WRITERS ON FISH AND FISHING, by R. B. Marston (1894).

IZAAK WALTON AND HIS FRIENDS, by Stapleton Martin (1903).

THOMAS KEN AND IZAAK WALTON, by E. Marston (1908).

IZAAK WALTON AND THE ROYAL DEANERY OF STAFFORD, by L. Lambert (1926).

THE DEVELOPMENT OF ENGLISH BIOGRAPHY, by H. Nicolson (1927).
Disparages Walton.

ENGLISH BIOGRAPHY BEFORE 1700, by D. A. Stauffer, Cambridge, Mass. (1930).
Contains a valuable chapter on Walton.

IZAAK WALTON'S METHODS IN BIOGRAPHY, by J. E. Butt (in *Essays and Studies of the English Association*, xix, 1934).

IZAAK WALTON'S COLLECTIONS FOR FULMAN'S LIFE OF JOHN HALES, by J. E. Butt (in *Modern Language Review*, xxix, 1934).

IZAAK WALTON'S HANDLING OF LETTERS, by R. E. Bennett (in *Philological Quarterly*, xvi, 1937).

LIFE OF IZAAK WALTON, by A. M. Coon, an unpublished Cornell University Ph.D. thesis. Abstracts of Cornell Univ. Theses 1938.

A NOTE ON REPRINTS

The Compleat Angler has been reprinted at least 289 times. The following editions are some of those which have special points of interest:

1750 Edited by M. Browne.

1760 Edited with biographical memoir by Sir J. Hawkins.

1823 Edited with introduction by J. Major.

1825 In Pickering's Diamond Classics.

1833 Edited by J. Rennie.

1836 Pickering, with memoir and notes by Sir H. Nicolas.

1847 Edited by G. W. Bethune.

1856 Bohn, edited by E. Jesse.

1878 In the Chandos Classics, edited by G. C. Davies.

1888 Lea & Dove edition, edited by R. B. Marston. Including *The Chronicle of The Complete Angler*, by T. Westwood and T. Satchell.

1889 Edited by J. R. Lowell.

1893 Tercentenary Edition, edited by J. E. Harting.

1896 Edited by A. Lang.

1897 Introduced by R. Le Gallienne.

1901 Edited with introduction by J. Buchan.

1902   Winchester edition, edited by G. A. Dewar, with an essay by Sir E. Gray.

1915   Clarendon Press, with introduction by A. B. Gough and notes by T. Balston.

1926   Kenkyusha English Classics. English text with copious notes in Japanese by Y. Okakura.

1931   Introduced by H. Williamson.

1939   In the Modern Library.

1939   Penguin Books.

The Lives:

1796   With notes, and the life of the author, by T. Zouch, York.

1817   Third edition of Zouch, 'to which is now first added *Love and Truth*'.

1827   Pickering's Diamond Classics.

1833   S.P.C.K. edition.

1857   With memoir of Izaak Walton by W. Dowling.

1884   Bohn's Illustrated Library, edited by A. H. Bullen.

1927   World's Classics, with introduction by G. Saintsbury.